CATHOLIC PUZZLES,

Word Games, and Brainteasers

MATT SWAIM

VOLUME
1

AVE MARIA PRESS **AVE** Notre Dame, Indiana

_____

Founded in 1865, Ave Maria Press is a ministry of the United States Province of Holy Cross.

www.avemariapress.com

Paperback: ISBN-13 978-1-59471-549-5

Cover image © iStockphoto.com.

Cover and text design by Christopher D. Tobin.

Printed and bound in the United States of America.

Introduction

It is the glory of God to conceal things, but the glory of kings is to search

things out.

—Proverbs 25:2

The human experience is marked by questions almost from the beginning. From the time we first breathe air, we feel the need to *know* things: What are my fingers for? Who are these people taking care of me? As we get older, we find that our existence is marked by a series of problem-solving scenarios, some simple, some complicated. Who is God? What is love? Where is the closest bathroom?

Some reading this might prefer that the answers to these questions (and many others like them) be handed out on a platter. Others, however, are more of the mind of G. K. Chesterton, who once wrote that "the riddles of God are more satisfying than the solutions of man." If you can relate to that sentiment, then maybe these puzzles are for you.

The following pages contain a variety of brainteasers and word games, some simple, others more advanced. Enjoy the mental exercise that they require—you may even learn a thing or two about your faith along the way. I hope you have as much fun solving them as I had creating them.

Anagram: US Cities with Bible Names

Rearrange the letters to form the name of a US city that is based on a place mentioned in the Bible.

Example: NO ALIEN HOBO = LEBANON, OHIO

1. AGREEING OATHS

2. GENERAL MOOS

3. A NAVY PANHANDLE HIPPIE SILL

4. CABANA SNOWFIELD RHYMER

5. SHRILL MATRIARCHAL NOON

6. WHOLEHEARTED BOA BREACH

7. CUT KNEE BAKERY

8. IMMENSE SHEEP NETS

9. LATEX BEANIES

10. AXE PAIN HORIZON

Code Scramble 1

Unscramble the names of plants mentioned in the Bible, then copy the letters in the numbered cells to the corresponding blanks below to reveal a quote from 1 Peter. Letters can correspond to more than one number, and a number may appear more than once in the quotation.

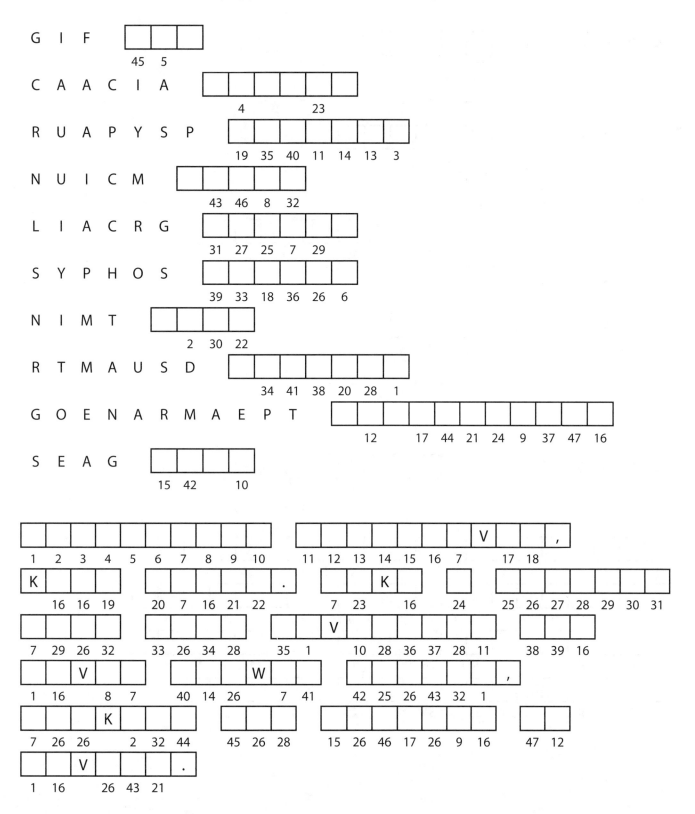

Code Scramble 2

Unscramble the names of plants mentioned in the Bible, then copy the letters in the numbered cells to the corresponding blanks below to reveal a quote from the book of James. Letters can correspond to more than one number, and numbers may appear more than once in the quotation.

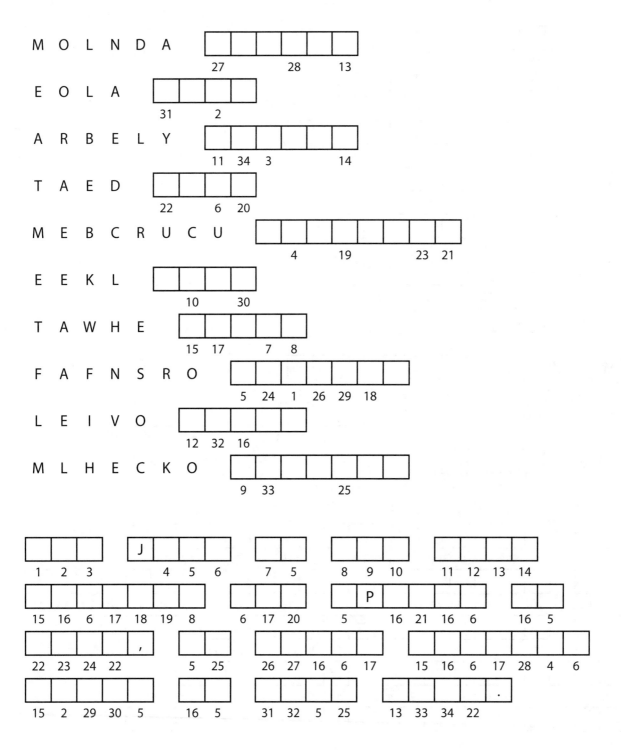

Code Scramble 3

Unscramble the names of places mentioned in the Bible, then copy the letters in the numbered cells to the corresponding blanks below to reveal a quote from the book of Psalms. Letters can correspond to more than one number, and numbers may appear more than once in the quotation.

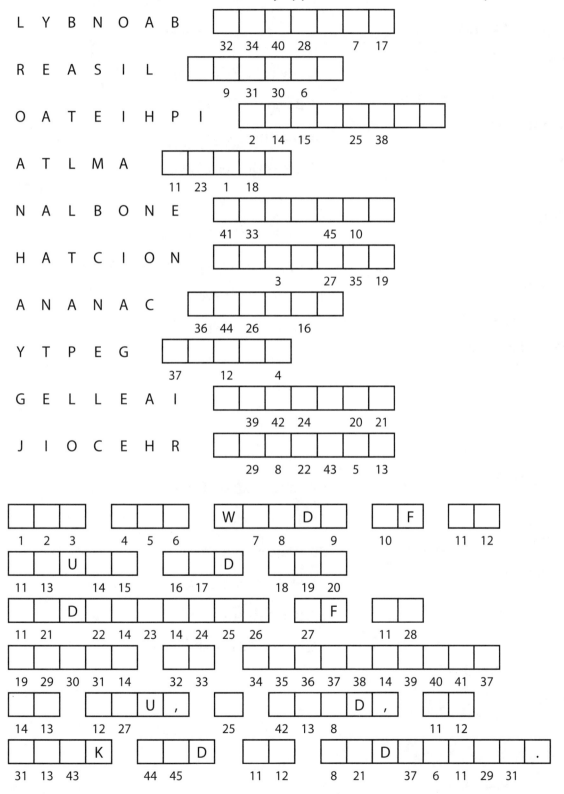

L Y B N O A B

32 34 40 28   7 17

R E A S I L

9 31 30 6

O A T E I H P I

2 14 15   25 38

A T L M A

11 23 1 18

N A L B O N E

41 33   45 10

H A T C I O N

3   27 35 19

A N A N A C

36 44 26   16

Y T P E G

37   12   4

G E L L E A I

39 42 24   20 21

J I O C E H R

29 8 22 43 5 13

---

1 2 3   4 5 6   W D   F   11 12
7 8 9   10

11 13 U 14 15   16 17 D   18 19 20

11 21 D 22 14 23 14 24 25 26   27 F   11 28

19 29 30 31 14   32 33   34 35 36 37 38 14 39 40 41 37

14 13   12 27 U ,   25   42 13 8 D ,   11 12

31 13 43 K   44 45 D   11 12   8 21 D 37 6 11 29 31 .

Word Link 1

Use the clues below to fill in the correct answers across and down. Each square will have one letter.

Across

1. Morning Prayer
4. Quintessential liturgical composer
5. Mass for the dead
8. Hermit
10. *Lamb*, in Latin
13. False oath
16. Home of St. Nicholas
17. German apostle
18. Pentecost liturgical color
19. Kidnapper of two popes
20. Patron of throats
22. Aloysius, in Italian
24. Overly self-critical
29. English Marian shrine
32. Lion leftover
34. Virtue's opposite
35. St. John Bosco's order
36. First baby
37. Sacred song
38. King David's usurping son
39. Primary English see

Down

2. Site of St. Paul's conversion
3. Bovine buffet
6. Franciscan or monkey
7. Greek Old Testament
9. Patron of eyes
11. France, previously
12. Religious community's book of the dead
14. Confession payoff
15. Deacon's outer vestment
21. Magi gift
23. Angela Merici's order
25. Diocesan division
26. Tithing herb
27. False accuser of English Catholics
28. Jesus' uncle
30. Angelic announcer
31. St Paul's hometown
32. Shoeless sister
33. Sea of Galilee, alternatively

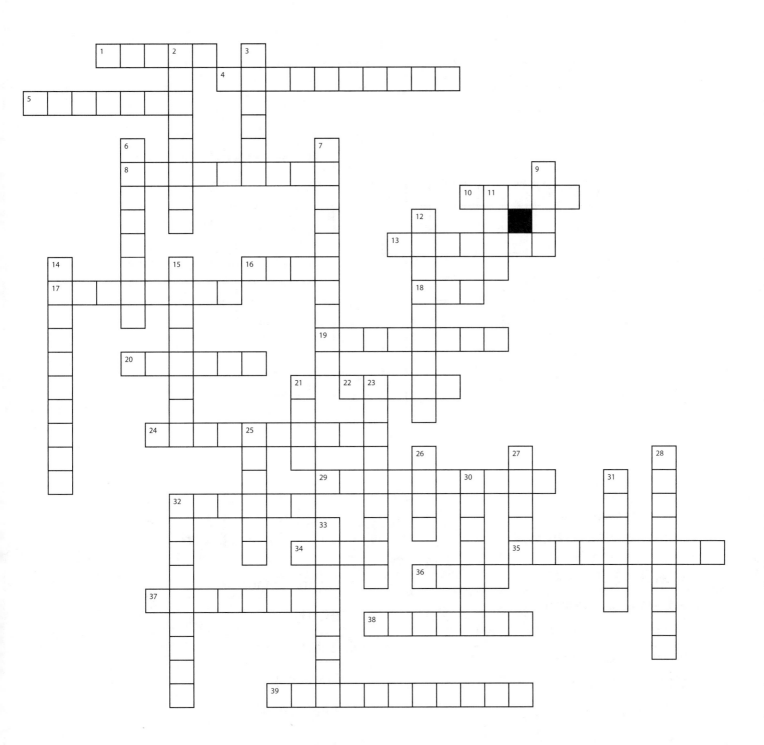

Word Link 2

Use the clues below to fill in the correct answers across and down. Each square will have one letter.

Across

3. Land of Esau
5. Goliath's hometown
7. "Faith of Our Fathers" composer
9. Galileo's last name
12. Moses's brother
13. Easter, in the East
14. Creedal council
15. First lady
17. Religious garb
18. Philistine deity
20. Light bearer

Down

1. Ten Commandments
2. YHWH
4. First US diocese
6. Saw or hat
8. Bridge builder
10. "Jesus fish"
11. Bishop's church
16. Staff
19. Crucifixion mount

Trial and Error

The list below contains the names of sixteen priests or religious from the field of science. Find a way to place them all in the correct horizontal or vertical blanks below so that each name is used and intersects properly with the rest. A brief explanation of who each person is follows their name.

Cantius	Developer of the theory of impetus
Consolmagno	Head of the Vatican Observatory
Copernicus	Champion of heliocentrism
Falloppio	Pioneering anatomist in women's medicine
Hengler	Inventor of the horizontal pendulum
Lemaître	Originator of the big bang theory
Mendel	Father of genetics
Mercalli	Developer of a scale that measures volcanic strength
Mersenne	Father of acoustics
Pacioli	Father of accounting
Picard	First to accurately measure Earth's size
Provancher	Canada's father of natural history
Ricci	Mathematician who wrote the first European-Chinese dictionary
Steno	Father of geology and stratigraphy
Verbiest	Designer of the first self-propelled vehicle
Vines	Developer of weather models that predict hurricane trajectory

Cryptofamily 1

The columns below are coded so that each letter represents another letter of the alphabet. For example, if *L* equals *T* in one of the words in a column, *L* will equal *T* for all the words in that column. Each of the three word groups, however, will have their own code. All the words in a given column will be related to the category header.

Categories of Sin	Animals Mentioned in the Bible	World Youth Day Sites
Example: Idolatry	*Example: Goat*	*Example: Panama City*
XBDT	HFLLE	NBGNTH
LSXXR	RXYVLT	SGJVEG
PJQGUBT	XJLY	SGABVA
JRGQMXST	RXDL	UZAJLZ
KSNRX	GIDLY	BTSL
JDJSNPX	NAHF	ITBTJIT
LWHHNK	RXB	XTETMJL
QGHM	GXXHPLG	YGBVU
KSXHGUKMNWB	WIPPOL	XOLUITXQTHG
LQGMMWBT	EAB	ALJKLB

Categories of Sin	Animals in the Bible	World Youth Day Sites
Example: Idolatry	*Example: Goat*	*Example: Panama City*
_____	_____	_____
_____	_____	_____
_____	_____	_____
_____	_____	_____
_____	_____	_____
_____	_____	_____
_____	_____	_____
_____	_____	_____
_____	_____	_____
_____	_____	_____

Cryptofamily 2

The columns below are coded so that each letter represents another letter of the alphabet. For example, if *L* equals *T* in one of the words in a column, *L* will equal *T* for all the words in that column. Each of the three word groups, however, will have their own code. All the words in a given column will be related to the category header.

Virtues	Women of the Bible	Tribes of Israel
Example: Generosity	*Example: Mary*	*Example: Reuben*
IHWVEVMS	MKGBP	FUVLIUOR
ITDLCMS	QIQ	CUF
QXHJLDBL	WKLUSUQWK	EUC
ITQL	JKUKW	UYLJB
YHCMVBL	BPJPKB	HKCUL
FOVMI	YVOPK	DUFUYYJL
FTXMVMHJL	UKMMKU	YRDJMF
MLWQLXODBL	SKJKU	RYYUNLUB
KXOMVMHJL	JQWQAKU	JVLBURD
QOMVLDBL	QYPNKWQLU	SJFHUDRF

Virtues

Example: Generosity

_____

_____

_____

_____

_____

_____

_____

_____

_____

Women of the Bible

Example: Mary

_____

_____

_____

_____

_____

_____

_____

_____

_____

Tribes of Israel

Example: Reuben

_____

_____

_____

_____

_____

_____

_____

_____

_____

Fallen Phrases 1

Drop the letters in each column down into the correct spaces in the puzzle to form a verse from the book of Proverbs.

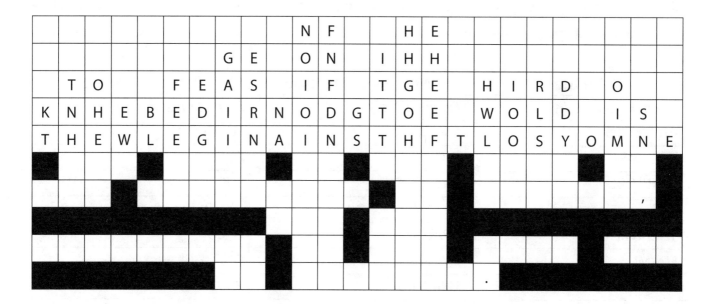

Fallen Phrases 2

Drop the letters in each column down into the correct spaces in the puzzle to form a verse from the book of Proverbs.

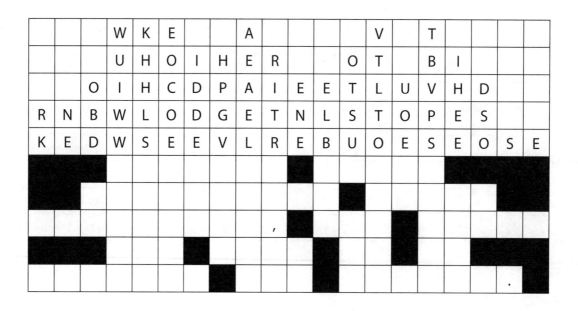

Fallen Phrases 3

Drop the letters in each column down into the correct spaces in the puzzle to form a verse from the book of Proverbs.

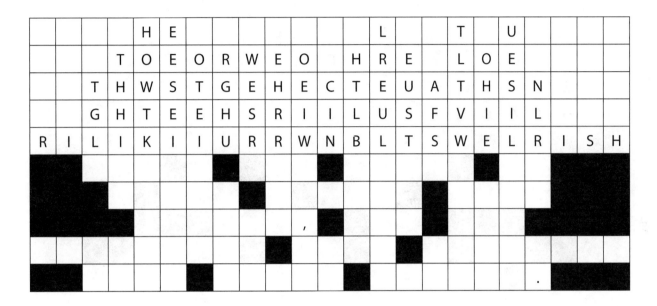

Fallen Phrases 4

Drop the letters in each column down into the correct spaces in the puzzle to form a verse from the book of Proverbs.

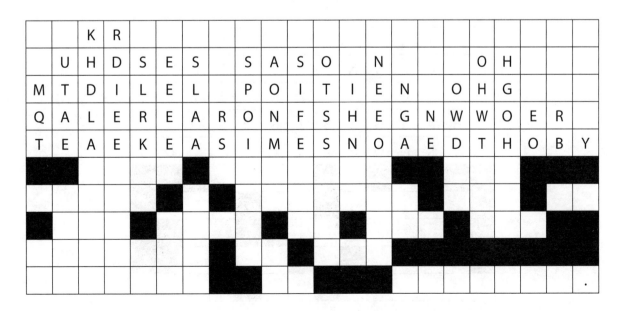

Fallen Phrases 5

Drop the letters in each column down into the correct spaces in the puzzle to form a verse from the book of Proverbs.

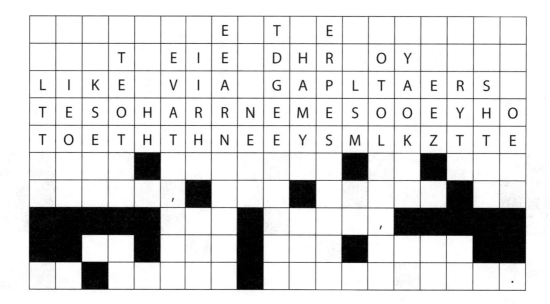

Fallen Phrases 6

Drop the letters in each column down into the correct spaces in the puzzle to form a verse from the book of Proverbs.

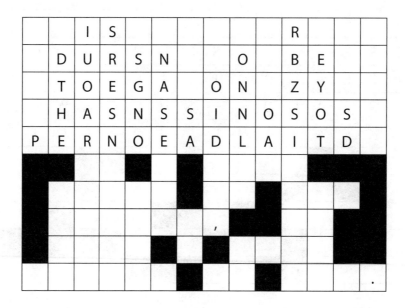

Fallen Phrases 7

Drop the letters in each column down into the correct spaces in the puzzle to form a verse from the book of Proverbs.

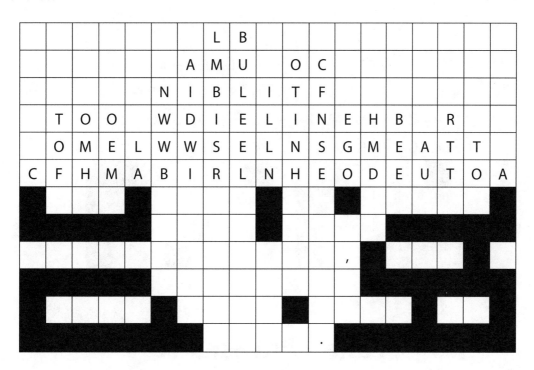

Fallen Phrases 8

Drop the letters in each column down into the correct spaces in the puzzle to form a verse from the book of Proverbs.

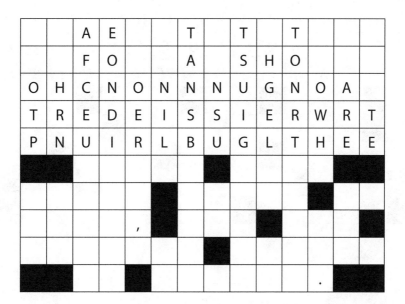

Fallen Phrases 9

Drop the letters in each column down into the correct spaces in the puzzle to form a verse from the book of Proverbs.

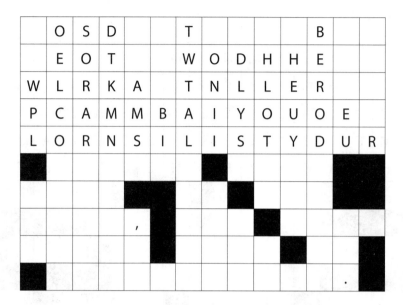

Fallen Phrases 10

Drop the letters in each column down into the correct spaces in the puzzle to form a verse from the book of Proverbs.

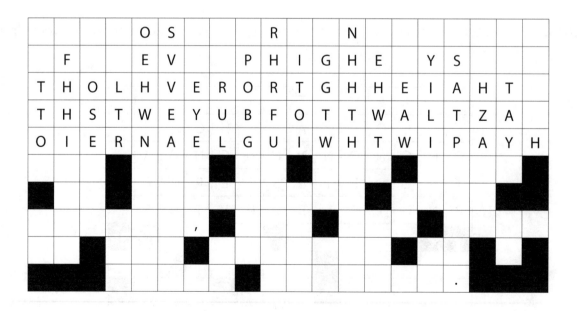

Fallen Phrases 11

Drop the letters in each column down into the correct spaces in the puzzle to form a verse from the book of Proverbs.

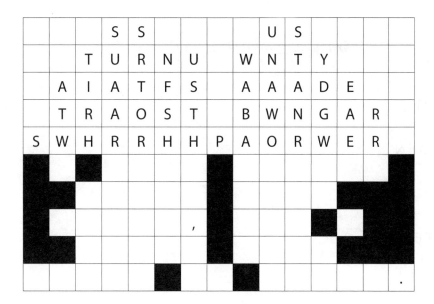

Fallen Phrases 12

Drop the letters in each column down into the correct spaces in the puzzle to form a verse from the book of Proverbs.

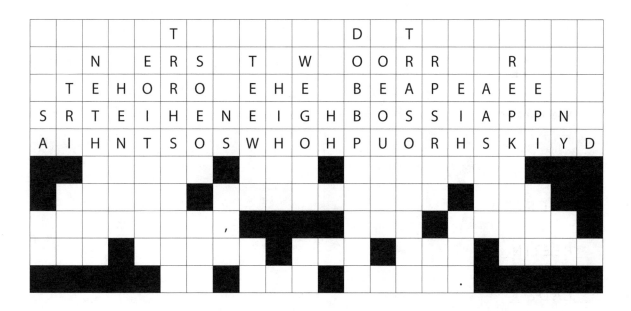

First and Last 1

The following list contains words that begin and end with the same letter. Each term relates to a person, object, or idea you might find or hear about inside a church.

Example:__ A T H O L I __ + C = CATHOLIC

1. __ L L E L U I __

2. __ E S T A M E N __

3. __ A N C T U __

4. __ A G I S T E R I U __

5. __ U R R E __

6. __ A F T E __

7. __ I T U R G I C A __

8. __ Y S T I C I S __

9. __ U __

10. __ D E E M E __

11. __ N A T H E M __

12. __ P I S T L __

13. __ P O C R Y P H __

14. __ R E E T I N __

15. __ E A D E __

16. __ R A N S E P __

First and Last 2

The following list contains saints' names that begin and end with the same letter.

Example: __ O L Y C A R __ + P = POLYCARP

1. __ I X T U __

2. __ N A S T A S I __

3. __ A V I __

4. __ G A T H __

5. __ U G __

6. __ D I L __

7. __ T A N I S L A U __

8. __ P O L L O N I __

9. __ Y A C I N T __

10. __ H I L I __

Hidden Humor 1

Find the names of popes in the puzzle, then place the remaining letters in the blanks below to form a biblical riddle. Words are hidden horizontally, vertically, and diagonally and are written both forward and backward.

```
N  E  H  P  E  T  S  U  I  R  A  L  I  H  W  E  S  X  A  C
H  E  E  V  A  R  I  S  T  U  S  U  I  P  L  T  I  R  N  O
E  W  A  V  I  G  I  L  I  U  S  S  S  E  E  L  M  O  A  R
B  E  N  E  D  I  C  T  L  O  S  M  U  L  E  S  P  O  S  N
M  A  R  C  E  L  L  I  N  U  S  T  E  F  S  U  L  N  T  E
S  A  B  I  N  I  A  N  T  S  H  S  C  P  U  H  I  M  A  L
A  L  E  X  A  N  D  E  R  E  P  A  N  E  I  C  C  A  S  I
G  A  I  U  S  T  P  S  R  H  I  D  A  L  S  A  I  R  I  U
R  E  E  M  P  A  L  I  O  U  E  S  I  A  Y  M  U  C  U  S
C  E  L  Z  G  S  U  R  S  T  O  I  H  G  N  M  S  E  S  T
S  A  T  A  O  S  U  Z  N  L  E  M  C  I  O  Y  T  L  H  N
U  E  L  S  S  A  N  E  S  E  R  Y  U  I  S  A  L  S  E
T  I  D  L  E  I  I  D  I  P  E  O  T  S  D  N  A  U  U  C
E  O  F  S  I  V  U  M  E  G  H  H  U  S  D  N  P  S  I  O
L  U  C  I  U  S  L  S  U  O  Y  Y  E  O  I  A  E  U  C  N
C  L  E  M  E  N  T  Y  U  S  D  H  R  C  O  B  T  R  I  N
S  I  L  V  E  R  I  U  S  C  L  A  E  I  I  R  E  E  R  I
S  U  I  R  E  B  I  L  S  O  R  T  T  U  N  U  R  T  I  M
E  C  A  F  I  N  O  B  O  N  U  A  S  U  S  U  H  N  S  E
C  E  L  E  S  T  I  N  E  S  D  A  M  A  S  U  S  A  A  D
```

Adeodatus	Agapetus	Alexander
Anastasius	Anicetus	Anterus
Benedict	Boniface	Caius
Callistus	Celestine	Clement
Cletus	Cornelius	Damasus
Dionysius	Eleutherius	Eusebius
Eutychian	Evaristus	Felix
Gaius	Gelasius	Hilarius
Hormisdas	Hyginus	Innocent
Lando	Leo	Liberius
Linus	Lucius	Marcellinus
Marcellus	Marcus	Pelagius
Peter	Pius	Sabinian
Silverius	Simplicius	Siricius
Soter	Stephen	Sylvester
Symmachus	Telesphorus	Urban
Vigilius	Zephyrinus	Zosimus

_ _ _ _ _ _ _ _ _ _ _ _ _ _ _ _ _ '_

_ _ _ _ _ _ _ ?

_ _ _ _ _ _ _ _ _ _ _

_ _ _ _ _ _ _ _ '_ _ _ _ _ _ .

Hidden Humor 2

Find the names of biblical professions in the puzzle, then place the remaining letters in the blanks below to form a biblical riddle. Words are hidden horizontally, vertically, and diagonally and are written both forward and backward.

```
R  C  N  E  B  I  R  C  S  W  R  T  H  Y  W
T  E  H  A  A  S  S  N  T  E  S  N  T  P  P
E  A  T  A  M  W  T  O  T  E  R  A  W  R  O
R  R  X  E  R  R  A  N  L  I  E  H  D  O  A
B  O  U  C  R  I  E  T  T  D  T  C  H  P  E
L  E  A  V  O  P  O  H  C  E  I  R  N  H  M
O  F  T  H  R  L  R  T  S  H  E  E  P  E  I
H  A  R  A  I  S  L  E  E  I  M  M  R  T  D
E  E  C  S  B  E  C  E  T  E  F  A  A  U  W
D  R  E  H  P  E  H  S  C  N  R  S  N  E  I
R  E  K  A  M  T  N  E  T  T  I  T  H  E  F
N  A  I  C  I  S  U  M  R  E  O  W  E  R  E
P  E  R  F  U  M  E  R  E  T  W  R  E  L  V
R  E  Y  W  A  L  E  A  R  A  L  O  H  C  S
P  O  S  G  A  R  D  E  N  E  R  T  L  E  S
```

Carpenter
Charioteer
Fisherman
Gardener
Interpreter
Lawyer
Merchant
Midwife
Musician
Perfumer
Prophet
Scholar
Scribe
Shepherd
Soldier
Tax Collector
Tentmaker
Watchman

___ _____ __ _____ _____

_____ ___ _____ __ ___

_____ ?

_____ _____ ____ _____

_____ .

Missing Vowels Word Search

To find the ten plagues of Egypt below, fill in the blanks with the missing vowels. Words are hidden horizontally, vertically, and diagonally and are written both forward and backward.

X	J	C	Q	W	G	D	Y	Q	K
T	H	M	H	T	S	N	G	W	C
R	N	T	D	L	L	_	_	H	_
N	L	Q	_	F	_	B	Q	T	T
J	T	V	R	C	_	C	F	X	S
G	X	_	K	N	B	L	K	M	
B	G	Y	N	V	_	L	H	L	V
S	Q	M	_	_	F	K	_	R	_
X	Q	G	S	T	S	_	C	_	L
F	_	R	S	T	B	_	R	N	D

Blood	Boils	Darkness	Firstborn	Flies
Frogs	Gnats	Hail	Livestock	Locusts

Work Search

Find the corporal and spiritual works of mercy hidden horizontally, vertically, and diagonally and written both forward and backward in this puzzle.

```
H Q A Y Y S S X E N Y O L K N M X L L T I W M C F
D W G L S T X R Y Y E O I S G O D H V Z F R I O X
K J P T M B Q L X V J Y F A N K D I P G J B R P R
E G V N C W C E K P V R I C E I S I W U L G V E A
M I I E L I M P P T G G O C N I K W H U I S N T M
T V S I O T Q Y A Z W N M X T F Z B F V R N L T Y
A E I T T Z X H N V I U H T E H B W E D I O O C R
O D T A H E V Y F Z L H H N H W O O Y S V M Q Y H
D R T P E X S H L K J E K A E R F C E U R V W Q C
C I H S T W G G O S S H E R R F O H S H N J A M Z
N N E G H N M S C I K T Z O E Y T O C D F U I Y N
U K I N E R A F C K G D S N I H H G Q M C D C A E
L T M O N A A K D Y Q E S G S C F V Z O T X B Q Y
G O P R A Y F O R T H E L I V I N G A N D D E A D
I T R W K G D V J T S F N E W Y B O Z S W S C A F
D H I R E N T D T W I O N H N W U E S Q M O K R N
L E S A D X V R I F M A J T C U R N P G X O K H T
P T O E Y A O L V D T L Z T O T Y F S Q G U V X L
J H N B B F L Q A O P U M C E L T K L H M P K X E
B I E L M I U W I Y M K Z U I P H Q Y U G Q F M Y
N R D O N S R S H E L T E R T H E H O M E L E S S
N S C G L K C O U N S E L T H E D O U B T F U L P
J T L R R X A E D C Y D H S R L E E U S A H T U Y
N Y P Y T N R B P L O N I N L K A V A T P Y T R R
J Q K J Z E G B P M B M F I M Z D L H L K D K S D
```

Corporal Works of Mercy

Feed the hungry

Give drink to the thirsty

Clothe the naked

Shelter the homeless

Visit the sick

Visit the imprisoned

Bury the dead

Spiritual Works of Mercy

Counsel the doubtful

Instruct the ignorant

Admonish the sinner

Comfort the sorrowful

Forgive offenses willingly

Bear wrongs patiently

Pray for the living and dead

Magic Word: Going to Church

Each of the nine clues below refers to a phrase, title, person, place, or thing that contains the word *church*.

1. *Sideways* actor

2. Murder mystery series starring David Tennant

3. Phrase meaning "noiseless"

4. Third largest city in New Zealand

5. British prime minister during World War II

6. Bottle or can opener

7. Dana Carvey character

8. Welsh singer

9. Home of "The Run for the Roses"

1. _____

2. _____

3. _____

4. _____

5. _____

6. _____

7. _____

8. _____

9. _____

Magic Word: Kindred Soul

The following clues refer to people, places, things, and phrases that contain the word *soul*.

1. Sam & Dave hit single
2. "Chopsticks" companion
3. *Hints Allegations and Things Left Unsaid* band
4. Subcompact station wagon
5. Arena football team
6. Inspirational short-story series
7. Tuft of facial hair
8. Beatles album
9. Humor advice in *Hamlet*
10. St. John of the Cross work

1. _____

2. _____

3. _____

4. _____

5. _____

6. _____

7. _____

8. _____

9. _____

10. _____

Message in the Middle 1

Write a letter in each blank that will form a common three-letter word with the letters above and below it. Note that some blanks can have more than one possible answer and that the same three-letter vertical word may appear more than once in the puzzle. When all the correct letters are filled in, a quote from the book of Romans will appear.

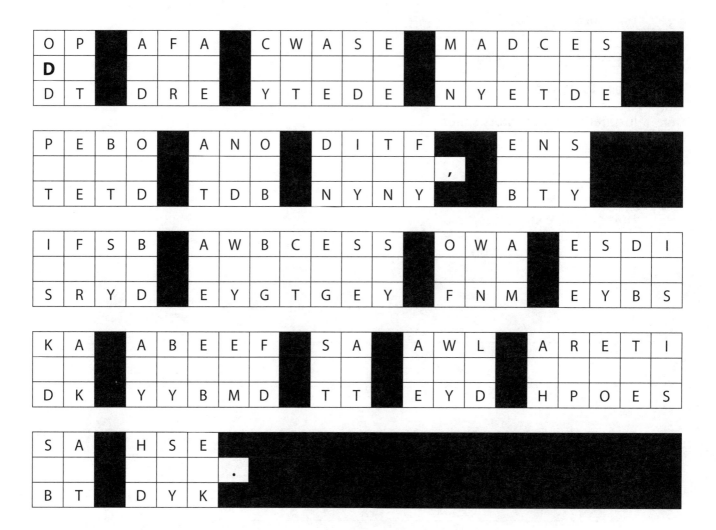

Message in the Middle 2

Write a letter in each blank that will form a common three-letter word with the letters above and below it. Note that some blanks can have more than one possible answer and that the same three-letter vertical word may appear more than once in the puzzle. When all the correct letters are filled in, a quote from 1 Corinthians will appear.

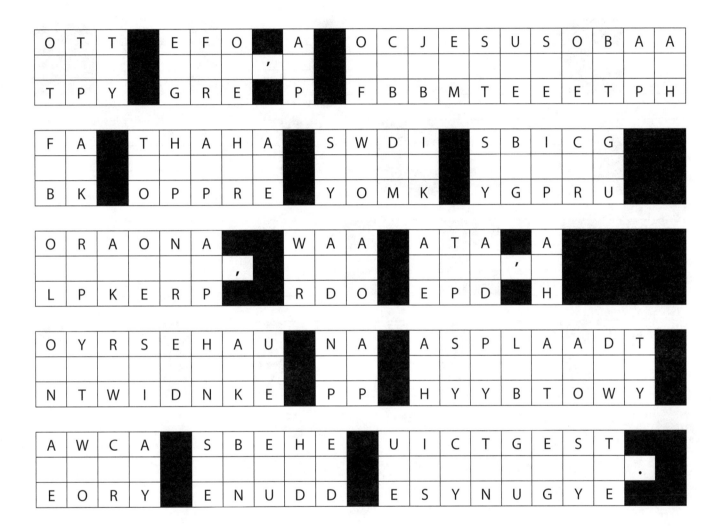

Message in the Middle 3

Write a letter in each blank that will form a common three-letter word with the letters above and below it. Note that some blanks can have more than one possible answer and that the same three-letter vertical word may appear more than once in the puzzle. When all the correct letters are filled in, a quote from 1 Corinthians will appear.

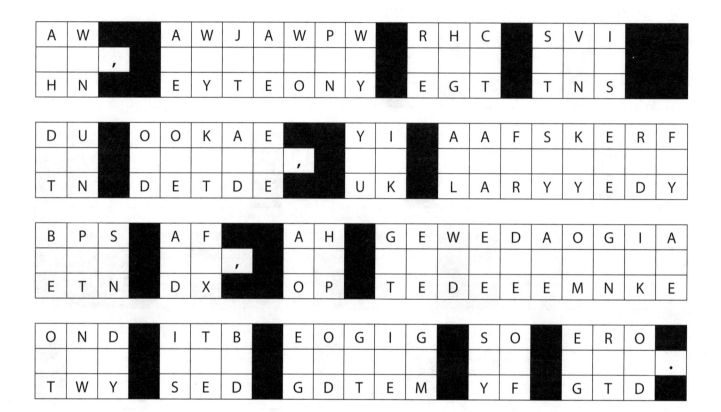

Message in the Middle 4

Write a letter in each blank that will form a common three-letter word with the letters above and below it. Note that some blanks can have more than one possible answer and that the same three-letter vertical word may appear more than once in the puzzle. When all the correct words are filled in, a quote from 1 Corinthians will appear.

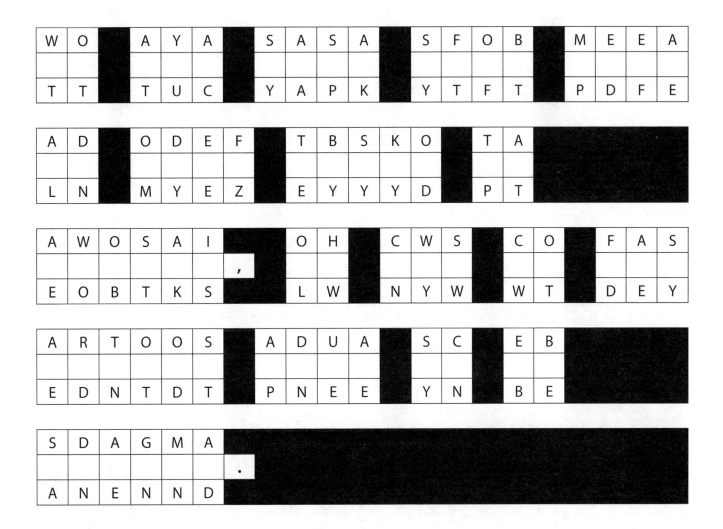

Missing Letter 1

One letter of the alphabet is missing from each box below. Write the missing letter on the blank beneath each box, then unscramble the missing letters to reveal the name of a pilgrimage site.

Y	A	F	I	X
G	V	K	O	C
B	M	D	R	S
J	Q	N	T	P
W	E	L	H	Z

Q	X	D	Z	U
A	J	R	H	F
G	V	O	M	S
L	Y	N	W	K
C	T	E	I	B

G	Q	M	D	S
C	N	J	T	I
U	X	B	V	O
K	Z	L	Y	R
F	W	P	E	H

_____   _____   _____

V	A	G	D	Y
F	J	Q	S	I
C	W	K	M	E
X	H	B	R	O
N	T	P	L	Z

O	T	A	V	Y
K	P	J	Z	B
S	Q	H	F	E
I	U	L	R	X
M	D	C	W	N

F	J	N	R	H
U	V	Z	W	K
Q	C	D	A	O
M	Y	B	X	S
I	T	P	L	G

_____   _____   _____

C	H	L	P	E
M	B	O	Y	Q
S	J	T	I	V
D	W	Z	X	N
K	U	G	R	F

I	G	S	C	P
H	T	N	Y	K
B	R	X	U	W
Q	L	F	Z	A
M	E	V	O	J

M	R	W	U	O
T	Q	Z	A	Y
X	E	G	I	K
H	B	J	N	D
P	C	V	F	S

_____   _____   _____

_____ _____ _____ _____ _____ _____ _____ _____ _____

Missing Letter 2

One letter of the alphabet is missing from each box below. Write the missing letter on the blank beneath each box, then unscramble the missing letters to reveal a book of the Bible.

I	R	V	Z	J
C	M	D	N	S
Y	G	Q	E	W
U	P	F	O	A
L	B	X	T	K

____

L	V	R	W	I
C	P	D	M	X
U	G	Q	E	S
B	O	F	N	Y
K	A	T	Z	J

____

E	O	K	P	G
Q	F	R	I	S
M	T	B	U	N
V	J	W	C	X
H	Y	L	Z	D

____

D	H	L	F	B
M	A	Q	O	R
S	U	X	G	J
E	T	W	Y	P
K	I	V	N	C

____

O	S	W	A	J
Z	P	E	K	Y
U	G	L	B	V
F	M	H	Q	D
N	C	X	T	R

____

E	I	M	Q	B
P	T	X	U	F
L	W	Z	Y	J
H	S	V	R	N
D	O	K	G	C

____

P	T	X	B	Q
A	E	I	F	U
W	L	M	J	Y
S	H	K	G	C
O	D	Z	V	R

____

Q	Z	D	H	T
K	U	L	W	A
G	O	Y	M	E
C	X	N	V	I
S	J	F	B	R

____

F	O	S	W	H
Z	J	A	K	P
V	C	N	D	T
R	M	B	L	X
I	Y	U	Q	G

____

__ __ __ __ __ __ __ __ __

Misspelled Books of the Bible

Add or delete a letter to correct the misspelled books of the Bible below, then write the added or deleted letter in the blank next to each word. Unscramble the letters at the bottom of the page to reveal the name of a Catholic pilgrimage destination.

1.   Philipians ___

2.   1 and 2 Macabees ___

3.   Galtians ___

4.   1 and 2 Thesalonians ___

5.   Mathew ___

6.   Geneosis ___

7.   1 and 2 Sammuel ___

8.   Phillemon ___

9.   Sireach ___

10.   Ezora ___

___ ___ ___ ___ ___ ___ ___ ___ ___

One or the Other 1

One letter from each vertical pair below is correct. Choose the correct letters to form a verse from the book of Sirach. The pairs are presented without spaces or punctuation.

P	U	T	S	E	W	H	L	A	E	S	P	E	C	T	P	H	E	I	D
T	H	O	N	L	R	Y	O	R	N	O	K	H	V	L	T	Y	M	S	R

L	A	N	C	E	Q	M	I	C	L	V	D	V	Z	S	Z	O	G	L	V
F	I	T	H	S	R	W	K	L	Y	H	A	R	E	L	O	N	H	R	I

T	E	C	N	D	C	H	O	S	E	D	H	O	G	P	C	O	F	C	N
F	F	A	L	Y	T	R	V	K	M	W	F	A	H	O	N	L	R	T	H

E	I	R	M	O	D	C	E	V	O	B	E	Z	S	H	F	L	N	P	D
L	M	Z	Y	N	T	H	I	R	U	E	L	Y	T	Y	E	M	O	R	A

_____

_____

_____

One or the Other 2

One letter from each vertical pair below is correct. Choose the correct letters to form a quotation from St. Aloysius Gonzaga. The pairs are presented without spaces or punctuation.

I	N	O	S	V	A	T	M	E	R	T	Y	B	O	I	C	O	L	L	H
A	T	I	R	B	E	L	T	O	S	V	O	S	E	A	D	H	I	P	D

O	A	R	O	D	C	H	A	S	K	B	N	A	R	F	N	H	O	W	T
B	F	G	N	A	T	L	E	N	U	I	M	G	O	I	T	E	E	C	H

O	G	O	N	O	L	L	D
A	L	E	W	A	R	D	O

_____

_____

Quote Solver 1

Solve the clues and match the letters to their corresponding numbers to reveal a quotation from St. Elizabeth Ann Seton.

1. Hive noise __ __ __ __
           21 12 22 22

2. Ubiquitous utensil __ __ __ __ __
              7 10 11 6 17

3. Job for sock sorters __ __ __ __ __ __ __ __
             20 13 1 19 2 5 8 18

4. To join metal parts __ __ __ __
           16 3 14 9

5. Horse or dragon __ __ __
         4 14 15

"__ __
 1 2 3   4 5 6 7 1   3 8 9   5   10 6 11 10 11 7 3   5 8   11 12 6

__ __
 9 13 5 14 15   16 11 6 17   5 7   1 11   9 11   1 2 3   16 5 14 14   11 4

__ __ __ ; __ __ __ __ __ __ __ __ , __ __ __ __ __ __ __ __ __ __
18 11 9   7 3 19 11 8 9 14 15   1 11   9 11   5 1   5 8   1 2 3

__ __ __ __ __ __ __ __ __ __ __ __ __ __ ; __ __ __ __ __ __ __ __ __ __ ,
20 13 8 8 3 6 2 3 16 5 14 14 7 5 1   13 8 9 1 2 5 6 9 14 15

__ . "
 1 11 9 11 5 1 21 3 19 13 12 7 3   5 1   5 7   2 5 7 16 5 14 14

Quote Solver 2

Solve the clues and match the letters to their corresponding numbers to reveal a quotation from St. Teresa of Calcutta.

1. Alert to danger __ __ __ __
                      1 2 3 4

2. Debunked legend __ __ __ __
                      5 6 2 7

3. Kitschy Elvis medium __ __ __ __ __ __
                      8 9 10 8 9 11

4. Dodgeball move __ __ __ __
                    12 13 14 15

5. Dictate __ __ __
              16 2 17

6. Pry open __ __ __ __ __
              18 19 20 20 17

7. Set a price __ __ __
              21 19 7

" __ , __ __ __
  1 5 9 4 17 6 13 10 6 6 15 2 11 11 5 9 14 3 13 14 19 21 19 7 17 6 13

__ __
13 4 12 9 3 16 11 2 4 12 5 6 1 20 13 14 5 18 9 16 13 16 10 6 8 9 12

__ __ __ __ __ __ __ ; __ __ __ __ __ __ __ __ __ __ __ __ __ __ __
17 6 13 11 5 9 4   1 5 9 4 17 6 13 10 6 6 15 2 11 11 5 9

__ __ __ __ __ __ __ __ __ __ , __ __ __ __ __ __ __ __ __ __ __ __ __ __
16 2 14 3 9 12 5 6 16 11 17 6 13 13 4 12 9 3 16 11 2 4 12 5 6 1

__ __ __ __ __ __ __ __ __ __ __ __ __ __ __ . "
20 13 14 5 5 9 10 6 8 9 16 17 6 13 4 6 1

Quote Tiles 1

Arrange the tiles below in the proper order to reveal a verse from 1 John. Each tile consists of three boxes containing letters, punctuation marks, and spaces; quotation marks are not included.

T	W	

W	;	

I	L	L

D	,	

K	E	

	H	A

	I	S

R	E	N

	C	H

	N	O

E	N	

	W	H

	I	S

K	N	O

	B	E

E	A	L

A	R	E

	B	E

D	O	

W	H	A

B	E	L

	L	I

	A	S

H	I	S

E		W

O	R	

V	E	A

,		F

I	L	L

W	E	

W		I

L	S	

R	E	V

I	L	D

S		T

O	T	

O	V	E

S		N

.		

:		W

,		W

D	'	S

E	E	

	R	E

L	E	D

E	D	.

A	T	

H	I	M

	G	O

W	I	L

W	E	

H	E	N

E		W

	B	E

W	E	

Y	E	T

	H	E

H	I	M

	H	E

Quote Tiles 2

Arrange the tiles below in the proper order to reveal a verse from 2 Peter. Each tile consists of three boxes containing letters, punctuation marks, and spaces; quotation marks are not included.

O	W			U	T			N	K			N	Y				W	I
B	U				T	O		T	H	E		A	T	I		N	O	T
W	A	N		E	N	T		U	T			S	L	O		M	E	
	A	S		S	E	,		I	S			P	E	R			P	R
T	O			Y	O	U		O	F			O	T			R	D	
	L	O		T	H	I		M	E			T	I	N		E	.	
A	B	O		I	S	H		W	N	E		T	H			O	M	I
G	A				S	O		T		I		S		P		R	E	P
S	S	,			C	O		H	I	S			S	L		E	N	T
,		N		T	O			A	N	C		,		B		A	L	L

(empty answer grid)

Scrambled Partner Saints

Unscramble the saints' names on each side of the puzzle, then draw a line to match the ones who are commonly mentioned together.

ASCMSO			DHSIEUOMT
YMRA			LAERC
IYLCR			LSHTOAISCAC
EETRP			USITT
SRICFNA			NIADMA
ESAMJ			NNAE
DETECBIN			ISEUUGATN
HYITTOM			SPJOHE
OAMCIN			HJNO
ICOMJAH			ULPA

Syllacrostics 1: Papal Encyclicals

Use the following syllables to assemble the Latin names of encyclicals issued by modern popes. The number following each clue tells how many syllables are in an encyclical's name. Each syllable will only be used once.

BREN CEM DA DE DEMP DER DES ET HO HU FI FI GE I IN LAU LU MA MEN MI MIT NAE NEN NIS NO NUM O PA RA RE RE RIS RUM RUM SAL SI SINT SOR SPE TAE TER TI TO TOR U UT VA VI VI

1. Foundational social justice document (5) __ __ __ __ __   __ __ __ __ __ __ __

2. Reinforced Church teaching on contraception (5) __ __ __ __ __ __ __   __ __ __ __ __

3. John Paul II's first encyclical (6) __ __ __ __ __ __ __ __   __ __ __ __ __ __

4. *On Care for Our Common Home* (4) __ __ __ __ __ __ __   __ __

5. Collaboration of Francis and Benedict XVI (4) __ __ __ __ __   __ __ __ __ __

6. John Paul II on ecumenism (4) __ __   __ __ __ __   __ __ __ __

7. Against the Nazis (6) __ __ __   __ __ __ __ __ __ __ __ __ __   __ __ __ __ __

8. John XXIII's final encyclical (5) __ __ __ __ __   __ __   __ __ __ __ __ __

9. "In hope we are saved" (3) __ __ __   __ __ __ __ __ __

10. John Paul II on faith and reason (6) __ __ __ __ __   __ __   __ __ __ __ __

Syllacrostics 2: American Saints, Blesseds, and Servants of God

Use the following syllables to assemble the names of American saints, blesseds, and servants of God. The number following each clue tells how many syllables are in a given person's name. Each syllable will only be used once.

BRI CA CA CENT CIS COR DAN DE EL ERRE FA HAW JOHN KA KA KWI MANN MO LEY NEU NI NO PAT PEY PI PO RA RI RICK RO RO ROSE SAINT STAN TE TE TER THA THER THER THORNE TON TOUS VIN WAL ZEK

1. Her shrine is near Denver, Colorado (5) __ __ __ __ __ __ __ __ __ __ __

2. Often depicted with a turtle (7) __ __ __ __ __ __ __ __ __ __ __ __ __ __

3. Referred to Niagara Falls as "my baptismal font" (3) __ __ __ __ __ __ __ __ __ __

4. Philanthropist and hairdresser (4) __ __ __ __ __ __ __ __ __ __ __ __ __

5. Killed in action in Vietnam (6) __ __ __ __ __ __ __ __ __ __ __ __ __

6. Daughter of a famous American novelist (3) __ __ __ __ __ __ __ __ __ __ __ __

7. Founder of public education in Puerto Rico (6) __ __ __ __ __ __ __ __ __ __ __ __

8. Russian prison camp survivor (4) __ __ __ __ __ __ __ __ __ __ __ __

9. Martyred by a Guatemalan death squad (4) __ __ __ __ __ __ __ __ __ __ __ __

10. Used Hollywood to promote the rosary (4) __ __ __ __ __ __ __ __ __ __ __

Syllacrostics 3: American Saints, Blesseds, and Servants of God

Use the following syllables to assemble the names of more American saints, blesseds, and servants of God. The number following each clue tells how many syllables are in a given person's name. Each syllable will only be used once.

A ANNE AU BETH BRU CA COPE DAY DE DO DORE E E GAL GUE GUS KA LA LIT LIZ MA ME MIL MO MON NUS O PAUN RE RI RIN RO SA SE SEY SI SO TE TE THE THER THY TOL TON TON TRI TUS US ZIN

1. His parents were freed slaves (5) __ __ __ __ __ __ __ __   __ __ __ __ __ __

2. Prisoner of war in Korea (4) __ __ __ __   __ __ __ __ __ __

3. Former Communist (4) __ __ __ __ __ __ __   __ __ __ __

4. French missionary to Indiana (5) __ __ __ __ __ __ __ __   __ __ __ __ __ __

5. Ran St. Joseph's Hospital in Syracuse, New York (4) __ __ __ __ __ __ __ __   __ __ __ __ __

6. Widow and religious order foundress (6) __ __ __ __ __ __ __ __ __   __ __ __ __ __ __

7. Made an honorary US citizen in 1996 (5) __ __ __ __ __ __   __ __ __ __ __ __

8. Michigan monastery doorkeeper (5) __ __ __ __ __ __ __ __   __ __ __ __ __

9. Former Russian prince (7) __ __ __ __ __ __ __ __ __   __ __ __ __ __ __ __ __

10. John Quincy Adams called him "the most learned American of his day"

    (4) __ __ __ __ __   __ __ __ __ __

What's Left? 1: St. Francis de Sales

Follow the steps below to reveal a quotation from St. Francis de Sales.

SOMETHING	NOTHING	EVERYTHING
READ	IS	DRIFTS
SO	DREAMS	STRONG
AS	GENTLENESS	TAKES
NOTHING	KEEPS	WHO
SO	LED	GENTLE
A	AS	REED
KNOB	CLOUDS	REAL
INSTEAD	STRENGTH	HEALS

1. Cross out the longest and shortest words in the first and third columns.
2. Cross out all verbs containing more than one vowel.
3. Cross off all words that are still words when spelled backward.
4. Cross off all words that rhyme with *said*.
5. Cross off all six-letter words whose middle four letters also form a word.

_____

_____

_____

What's Left? 2: Padre Pio

Follow the instructions below to reveal a quotation from St. Pio of Pietrelcina.

ATTEND	MY	SOLACE
PAST	WHEN	O
LORD	TO	ADDED
ANY	YOUR	ACQUIT
MERCY	MY	GRAND
WHENEVER	WHEN	PRESENT
WHO	TO	ONLY
GREAT	YOUR	LOVE
ENSURE	MY	AVAILABLE
FUTURE	TO	LARGE
INFORM	YOUR	YOU
PROVIDENCE	EVERY	PURSUE

1. Cross off every word that has the same letter three times.
2. Cross off every word that means "big."
3. Cross off every word that begins with a vowel and ends with a *y*.
4. Cross off every word in the middle column that occurs less than three times.
5. Cross off every word that rhymes with *new*.
6. Cross off every six-letter word that is still a word when you remove the first two letters.

_____

_____

_____

What's Left? 3: Pope Paul VI

Follow the instructions below to reveal a quotation from Pope Paul VI.

WE	HEARD	FIRST
ATTEMPT	MUST	WHEN
SEE	TO	HEIGHT
IT	THAT	ENTHUSIASM
THE	FOR	LISTEN
CROSSES	FORE	THE
FUTURE	STUNNED	DOES
NOT	OWNED	BOARD
BREED	GIVE	RISE
TO	DEFY	BABBLE
THE	CONTEMPT	LIGHT
FOR	THE	WHEN
PAST	NONE	BARRIERS

1. Cross off any word that appears twice in a column.
2. Cross off any word that is a number or ends in a number (e.g., *sleight* ends in *eight*).
3. Cross off any words that can be combined with the word *head* to form a new word.
4. Cross off any five-letter word that is still a word when you remove the middle letter.
5. Cross off any words that contain three consecutive letters of the alphabet.
6. Cross off all words that contain the same letter three times.

_____

_____

_____

Where Do the Consonants Go? 1: Ancestors of Jesus

Use the consonants from the word bank to reveal the names of some of Jesus' ancestors.

B DDDD HHHHH JJJ L MMMM NN P R SSSSSS T V

1. __ O __ O __ O __

2. A __ __ A __ A __

3. __ U __ A __

4. A __ A __

5. __ E __ __ E

6. __ E __ __

7. __ A __ I __

8. __ O A __

9. __ __ E __

10. __ O __ E __ __

Where Do the Consonants Go? 2: Devotions

Use the consonants from the word bank to reveal words associated with sacramentals and devotions.

CCCCCC DD F GG LLLLL MMM NNNNN PPP RRRRRR SSSSSS V X Y

1. __ A __ __ __ E __

2. __ __ A __ U __ A __

3. __ O __ E __ A

4. __ I __ __ __ I __ A __ E

5. __ E __ I __

6. __ O __ A __ __

7. __ A __ __ __

8. __ E __ A __ __

9. I __ __ E __ __ E

10. __ __ U __ I __ I __

Where Do the Consonants Go? 3: Lent

Use the consonants from the word bank to reveal words associated with Lent.

B CCC D FF GGG HH LL M NNNNNN PPPP RRRRR SSSSSSSS TTT V Y

1. A __ __ __ __ I __ I __ __

2. __ U __ __ __ E

3. A __ __ E __

4. __ A __ __ I __ __

5. __ E __ A __ __ E

6. A __ __ __ I __ E __ __ E

7. __ __ A __ E __

8. __ E __ E __ __

9. __ I __ __

10. __ __ O __ __

Where Do the Consonants Go? 4: Mysteries of the Rosary

Use the consonants from the word bank to reveal the names of the Mysteries of the Rosary.

CCCCC D FF GGG H M NNNNNNNNNNNNNNNNNNN PP RRRRRRRR
SSSSSSSS TTTTTTTTTTTT VV X YY

1. A _ O _ _ I _ _ _ _ E _ A _ _ E _

2. _ _ A _ _ _ _ I _ U _ A _ I O _

3. A _ _ U _ _ I A _ I O _

4. _ _ U _ I _ I _ I O _

5. _ I _ I _ A _ I O _

6. A _ _ E _ _ I O _

7. _ E _ U _ _ E _ _ I O _

8. _ _ E _ E _ _ A _ I O _

9. _ A _ I _ I _ _

10. A _ _ U _ _ _ I O _

Wordfalls 1: Fulton J. Sheen

Drop the words in each column into the proper spaces below to form a quote from Archbishop Fulton J. Sheen. One word from each column is a decoy.

NEVER	INVOLVING	SOUGHT	SAY	WRONG	MAN
COUNSEL	DOES	LOVE	AND	FOR	PRAYERS
EVERY	BE	NOT	WISDOM	A	SHOULD
WHO	DESIGN	RIGHT	FROM	HIS	HEART

Wordfalls 2: John Henry Newman

Drop the words in each column into the proper spaces below to form a quote from Bl. John Henry Newman. One word from each column is a decoy.

BUT	HAS	OF	THE	OF	EXCESS	SUBSTANCE
EVIL	CORRUPTION	ONLY	SUBSTANCE	DEFECT	ITS	PERVERSION
GRATITUDE	HAVEN	LIST	GROWTH	WHICH	GRACE	OWN
OR	IS	NO	THAT	DIVINE	HAS	NATURE

Wordfalls 3: Sirach

Drop the words in each column into the proper spaces below to form a quote from the book of Sirach. One word from each column is a decoy.

STRETCHED	NOT	IS	RECEIVE	HAND	CLOSED
DO	OUT	GRACE	YOUR	TO	BE
HEAVEN	IT	LET	DO	WITH	GIVE
WHEN	LOVE	TO	TIME	AND	PRAISE

What Are the Odds?

Fill in every other letter to reveal the names of towns visited by Jesus in the gospels.

1. N __ Z __ R __ T __

2. G __ L __ L __ E

3. C __ P __ R __ A __ U __

4. C __ N __

5. J __ R __ S __ L __ M

6. B __ T __ L __ H __ M

7. B __ T __ A __ Y

8. D __ C __ P __ L __ S

9. G __ N __ E __ A __ E __

10. B __ T __ S __ I __ A

11. C __ O __ A __ I __

12. E __ M __ U __

Alphabet Fill-Ins

Insert a different letter of the alphabet into each of the empty boxes below to complete a word that reads across. Each letter of the alphabet will only be used once. Not all of the letters in each row are necessary to form your word, and the letter you use may be the first or last letter of the answer or somewhere in the middle.

M	N	C	O	N	*F*	E	S	S	B	V
A	Z	X	G	E		E	S	I	S	C
S	D	H	E	A		E	N	F	G	H
C	O	L	L	E		E	P	L	K	J
O	I	U	R	E		U	I	E	M	Y
M	Q	W	C	H		I	R	E	R	T
N	B	B	I	S		O	P	V	C	X
D	S	A	B	A		T	I	S	M	Z
F	G	H	T	R		N	I	T	Y	J
I	O	P	V	I		T	U	E	L	K
U	Y	T	R	E		I	S	D	O	M
C	V	B	N	M		L	M	S	Q	W
X	Z	A	A	M		N	S	D	F	G
U	I	O	P	L		O	Y	K	J	H
Y	T	R	M	I		S	I	O	N	E
N	M	C	R	O		I	E	R	Q	W
B	V	C	B	I		L	E	X	Z	A
H	G	F	D	S		N	E	E	L	S
J	K	L	E	N		L	P	O	I	U
R	O	S	A	R		W	E	R	T	Y
Q	M	N	D	O		O	L	O	G	Y
C	V	B	H	O		I	N	E	S	S
X	Z	M	N	B		R	E	E	D	V
L	K	J	H	O		I	L	Y	H	G
F	D	L	I	T		R	G	Y	S	A
P	P	A	R	A		I	S	E	O	I

ANSWER KEYS

Anagram: US Cities with Bible Names

1. Athens, Georgia
2. Salem, Oregon
3. Philadelphia, Pennsylvania
4. New Smyrna Beach, Florida
5. Mars Hill, North Carolina
6. Rehoboth Beach, Delaware
7. Berea, Kentucky
8. Memphis, Tennessee
9. Abilene, Texas
10. Phoenix, Arizona

Code Scramble 1

FIG
ACACIA
PAPYRUS
CUMIN
GARLIC
HYSSOP
MINT
MUSTARD
POMEGRANATE
SAGE

"Discipline yourselves, keep alert. Like a roaring lion your adversary the devil prowls around, looking for someone to devour." (1 Peter 5:8)

Code Scramble 2

ALMOND
ALOE
BARLEY
DATE
CUCUMBER
LEEK
WHEAT
SAFFRON
OLIVE
HEMLOCK

"For just as the body without the spirit is dead, so faith without works is also dead." (James 2:26)

Code Scramble 3

BABYLON
ISRAEL
ETHIOPIA
MALTA
LEBANON
ANTIOCH
CANAAN
EGYPT
GALILEE
JERICHO

"Let the words of my mouth and the meditation of my heart be acceptable to you, O LORD, my rock and my redeemer." (Psalm 19:14)

Word Link 1

Cryptofamily 1

Categories of Sin

1. Envy
2. Greed
3. Calumny
4. Adultery
5. Pride
6. Avarice
7. Gossip
8. Lust
9. Presumption
10. Gluttony

Animals Mentioned in the Bible

1. Sheep
2. Donkey
3. Oxen
4. Dove
5. Raven
6. Fish
7. Dog
8. Rooster
9. Cattle
10. Pig

World Youth Day Sites

1. Krakow
2. Manila
3. Madrid
4. Sydney
5. Rome
6. Toronto
7. Cologne
8. Paris
9. Czestochowa
10. Denver

Cryptofamily 2

Virtues

1. Humility
2. Honesty
3. Prudence
4. Hope
5. Justice
6. Faith
7. Fortitude
8. Temperance
9. Gratitude
10. Patience

Women of the Bible

1. Naomi
2. Eve
3. Bathsheba
4. Rahab
5. Miriam
6. Lydia
7. Hannah
8. Sarah
9. Rebekah
10. Elizabeth

Tribes of Israel

1. Naphtali
2. Dan
3. Gad
4. Asher
5. Judah
6. Manasseh
7. Simeon
8. Issachar
9. Ephraim
10. Benjamin

Fallen Phrases 1

"The fear of the LORD is the beginning of wisdom, and the knowledge of the Holy One is insight." (Proverbs 9:10)

Fallen Phrases 2

"Whoever loves discipline loves knowledge, but those who hate to be rebuked are stupid." (Proverbs 12:1)

Fallen Phrases 3

"Those who trust in their riches will wither, but the righteous will flourish like green leaves." (Proverbs 11:28)

Fallen Phrases 4

"Like someone who takes a passing dog by the ears is one who meddles in the quarrel of another." (Proverbs 26:17)

Fallen Phrases 5

"Like vinegar to the teeth, and smoke to the eyes, so are the lazy to their employers." (Proverbs 10:26)

Fallen Phrases 6

"As a door turns on its hinges, so does a lazy person in bed." (Proverbs 26:14)

Fallen Phrases 7

"The wise of heart will heed commandments, but a babbling fool will come to ruin." (Proverbs 10:8)

Fallen Phrases 8

"Fools show their anger at once, but the prudent ignore an insult." (Proverbs 12:16)

Fallen Phrases 9

"Commit your work to the Lord, and your plans will be established." (Proverbs 16:3)

Fallen Phrases 10

"The way of the lazy is overgrown with thorns, but the path of the upright is a level highway." (Proverbs 15:19)

Fallen Phrases 11

"A soft answer turns away wrath, but a harsh word stirs up anger." (Proverbs 15:1)

Fallen Phrases 12

"Those who despise their neighbors are sinners, but happy are those who are kind to the poor." (Proverbs 14:21)

First and Last 1

1. Alleluia
2. Testament
3. Sanctus
4. Magisterium
5. Turret
6. Rafter
7. Liturgical
8. Mysticism
9. Nun
10. Redeemer
11. Anathema
12. Epistle
13. Apocrypha
14. Greeting
15. Reader
16. Transept

First and Last 2

1. Sixtus
2. Anastasia
3. David
4. Agatha
5. Hugh
6. Odilo
7. Stanislaus
8. Apollonia
9. Hyacinth
10. Philip

Hidden Humor 1

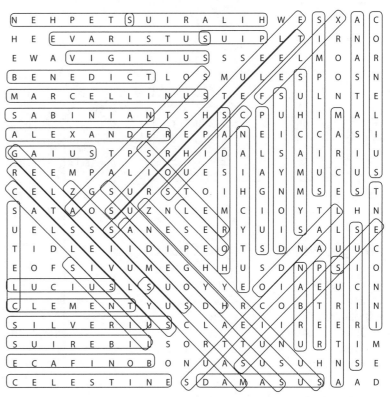

Where was Solomon's Temple? On the side of Solomon's head.

Hidden Humor 2

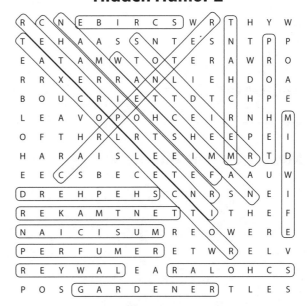

Why wasn't St. Peter worried about the leaven of the Pharisees?
Because there were twelve apostles.

Missing Vowels Word Search

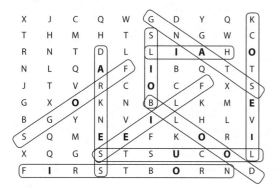

Magic Word: Going to Church

1. Thomas Haden Church
2. Broadchurch
3. "Quiet as a church mouse"
4. Christchurch
5. Winston Churchill
6. Church key
7. Church Lady
8. Charlotte Church
9. Churchill Downs

Magic Word: Kindred Soul

1. "Soul Man"
2. "Heart and Soul"
3. Collective Soul
4. Kia Soul
5. Philadelphia Soul
6. *Chicken Soup for the Soul*
7. Soul patch
8. *Rubber Soul*
9. "Brevity is the soul of wit"
10. *Dark Night of the Soul*

Work Search

```
H Q A Y Y S S X E N Y O L K N M X L L T I W M C F
D W G L S T X R Y Y E O I S G O D H V Z F R I O X
K J P T M B Q L X V J Y F A N K D I P G J B R P R
E G V N C W C E K P V R I C E I S I W U L G V E A
M I I E L I M P P T G G O C N I K W H U I S N T M
T V S I O T Q Y A Z W M X T F Z B F V R N L T Y
A E I T Z X H N V I U H T E H B W E D I O O C R
O D T A H E V Y F Z L H H N H W O O Y S M Q Y H
D R T P E X S H L K J E K A E R F C E U R V W Q S
C I H S T W G G O S S H E R R F O H S H N J A M Z
N N E G H N M S C I K T Z O E Y T O C D F U I Y N
U K I N E R A F C K D S N I H G Q M C D C A E
L T M O N A A K D Y Q E S C F V Z O T X B Q Y
G O P R A Y F O R T H E L I V I N G A N D D E A D
I T R W K G D V J T S F N E W Y B O Z S W S C A F
D H I R E N T D T W I O N H N W U E S Q M O K R N
L E S A D X V R I F M A J T C U R N P G X K H T
P T O E Y A O D L V D T L Z T O T Y F S Q U V X L
J H N B B F L Q A O P U M C E L T K L H M K X E
B I E L M I U W I Y M K Z U I P H Q Y U G Q F M Y
N R D O N S R S H E L T E R T H E H O M E L E S S
N S C G L K C O U N S E L T H E D O U B T F U L P
J T L R R X A E D C Y D H S R L E E U S A H T U Y
N Y P Y T N R B P L O N I N L K A V A T P Y T R R
J Q K J Z E G B P M B M F I M Z D L H L K D K S D
```

Message in the Middle 1

O P	A F A	C W A S E	M A D C E S
DO	**NOT**	**REPAY**	**ANYONE**
D T	D R E	Y T E D E	N Y E T D E

P E B O	A N O	D I T F	E N S
EVIL	**FOR**	**EVIL,**	**BUT**
T E T D	T D B	N Y N Y	B T Y

I F S B	A W B C E S S	O W A	E S D I
TAKE	**THOUGHT**	**FOR**	**WHAT**
S R Y D	E Y G T G E Y	F N M	E Y B S

K A	A B E E F	S A	A W L	A R E T I
IS	**NOBLE**	**IN**	**THE**	**SIGHT**
D K	Y Y B M D	T T	E Y D	H P O E S

S A	H S E
OF	**ALL.**
B T	D Y K

Romans 12:17

Message in the Middle 2

O T T	E F O	A	O C J E S U S O B A A
FOR	**GOD'S**	**FOOLISHNESS**
T P Y	G R E	P	F B B M T E E E T P H

F A	T H A H A	S W D I	S B I C G
IS	**WISER**	**THAN**	**HUMAN**
B K	O P P R E	Y O M K	Y G P R U

O R A O N A	W A A	A T A	A
WISDOM,	**AND**	**GOD'S**
L P K E R P	R D O	E P D H

O Y R S E H A U	N A	A S P L A A D T
WEAKNESS	**IS**	**STRONGER**
N T W I D N K E	P P	H Y Y B T O W Y

A W C A	S B E H E	U I C T G E S T
THAN	**HUMAN**	**STRENGTH.**
E O R Y	E N U D D	E S Y N U G Y E

1 Corinthians 1:25

Message in the Middle 3

SO, WHETHER YOU EAT OR DRINK, OR WHATEVER YOU DO, DO EVERYTHING FOR THE GLORY OF GOD.

1 Corinthians 10:31

Message in the Middle 4

IF FOR THIS LIFE ONLY WE HAVE HOPED IN CHRIST, WE ARE OF ALL PEOPLE MOST TO BE PITIED.

1 Corinthians 15:19

Missing Letter 1

U P A
U G E
A D L
GUADALUPE

Missing Letter 2

H H A
Z I A
N P E
ZEPHANIAH

Misspelled Books of the Bible

1. Philippians: P
2. 1 and 2 Maccabees: C
3. Galatians: A
4. 1 and 2 Thessalonians: S
5. Matthew: T
6. Genesis: O
7. 1 and 2 Samuel: M
8. Philemon: L
9. Sirach: E
10. Ezra: O

COMPOSTELA

One or the Other 1

"Those who respect their father will have long life, and those who honor their mother obey the Lord." (Sirach 3:6)

One or the Other 2

"It is better to be a child of God than king of the whole world." (St. Aloysius Gonzaga)

Quote Tiles 1

"Beloved, we are God's children now; what we will be has not yet been revealed. What we do know is this: when he is revealed, we will be like him, for we will see him as he is." (1 John 3:2)

Quote Tiles 2

"The Lord is not slow about his promise, as some think of slowness, but is patient with you, not wanting any to perish, but all to come to repentance." (2 Peter 3:9)

Quote Solver 1

1. Buzz
2. Spork
3. Matching
4. Weld
5. Fly

"The first end I propose in our daily work is to do the will of God; secondly, to do it in the manner he wills it; and thirdly, to do it because it is his will." (St. Elizabeth Ann Seton)

Quote Solver 2

1. Warn
2. Hoax
3. Velvet
4. Duck
5. Say
6. Jimmy
7. Fix

"When you look at the crucifix, you understand how much Jesus loved you then; when you look at the sacred host, you understand how much he loves you now." (St. Teresa of Calcutta)

Scrambled Partner Saints

Cosmas and Damian
Mary and Joseph
Cyril and Methodius
Peter and Paul
Francis and Clare
James and John
Benedict and Scholastica
Timothy and Titus
Monica and Augustine
Joachim and Anne

Syllacrostics 1: Papal Encyclicals

1. *Rerum Novarum*
2. *Humanae Vitae*
3. *Redemptor Hominis*
4. *Laudato Si'*
5. *Lumen Fidei*
6. *Ut Unum Sint*
7. *Mit Brennender Sorge*
8. *Pacem in Terris*
9. *Spe Salvi*
10. *Fides et Ratio*

Syllacrostics 2: American Saints, Blesseds, and Servants of God

1. Mother Cabrini
2. Kateri Tekakwitha
3. John Neumann
4. Pierre Toussaint
5. Vincent Capodanno
6. Rose Hawthorne
7. Rafael Cordero
8. Walter Ciszek
9. Stanley Rother
10. Patrick Peyton

Syllacrostics 3: American Saints, Blesseds, and Servants of God

1. Augustus Tolton
2. Emil Kapaun
3. Dorothy Day
4. Théodore Guérin
5. Marianne Cope
6. Elizabeth Seton
7. Mother Teresa
8. Solanus Casey
9. Demetrius Gallitzin
10. Simon Brute

What's Left? 1: St. Francis de Sales

"Nothing is so strong as gentleness, nothing so gentle as real strength."

What's Left? 2: Padre Pio

"My past, O Lord, to your mercy; my present to your love; my future to your providence."

What's Left? 3: Pope Paul VI

"We must see to it that enthusiasm for the future does not give rise to contempt for the past."

Where Do the Consonants Go? 1: Ancestors of Jesus

1. Solomon
2. Abraham
3. Judah
4. Adam
5. Jesse
6. Seth
7. David
8. Noah
9. Shem
10. Joseph

Where Do the Consonants Go? 2: Devotions

1. Candles
2. Scapular
3. Novena
4. Pilgrimage
5. Relic
6. Rosary
7. Palms
8. Medals
9. Incense
10. Crucifix

Where Do the Consonants Go? 3: Lent

1. Almsgiving
2. Purple
3. Ashes
4. Fasting
5. Penance
6. Abstinence
7. Prayer
8. Desert
9. Fish
10. Cross

Where Do the Consonants Go? 4: Mysteries of the Rosary

1. Agony in the Garden
2. Transfiguration
3. Annunciation
4. Crucifixion
5. Visitation
6. Ascension
7. Resurrection
8. Presentation
9. Nativity
10. Assumption

Wordfalls 1: Fulton J. Sheen

"Counsel involving right and wrong should never be sought from a man who does not say his prayers."

Wordfalls 2: John Henry Newman

"Evil has no substance of its own, but is only the defect, excess, perversion or corruption of that which has substance."

Wordfalls 3: Sirach

"Do not let your hand be stretched out to receive and closed when it is time to give." (Sirach 4:31)

What Are the Odds?

1. Nazareth
2. Galilee
3. Capernaeum
4. Cana
5. Jerusalem
6. Bethlehem
7. Bethany
8. Decapolis
9. Gennesaret
10. Bethsaida
11. Chorazin
12. Emmaus

Alphabet Fill-Ins

M	N	C	O	N	F	E	S	S	S	B	V
A	Z	X	G	E	N	E	S	I	S		C
S	D	H	E	A	V	E	N	F	G	H	
C	O	L	L	E	G	E		P	L	K	J
O	I	U	R	E	Q	U	I	E	M	Y	
M	Q	W	C	H	O	I	R	E	R	T	
N	B	B	I	S	H	O	P	V	C	X	
D	S	A	B	A	P	T	I	S	M	Z	
F	G	H	T	R	I	N	I	T	Y	J	
I	O	P	V	I	R	T	U	E	L	K	
U	Y	T	R	E	W	I	S	D	O	M	
C	V	B	N	M	A	L	M	S	Q	W	
X	Z	A	A	M	E	N	S	D	F	G	
U	I	O	P	L	J	O	Y	K	J	H	
Y	T	R	M	I	S	S	I	O	N	E	
N	M	C	R	O	Z	I	E	R	Q	W	
B	V	C	B	I	B	L	E	X	Z	A	
H	G	F	D	S	K	N	E	E	L	S	
J	K	L	E	N	T	L	P	O	I	U	
R	O	S	A	R	Y	W	E	R	T	Y	
Q	M	N	D	O	X	O	L	O	G	Y	
C	V	B	H	O	L	I	N	E	S	S	
X	Z	M	N	B	C	R	E	E	D	V	
L	K	J	H	O	M	I	L	Y	H	G	
F	D	L	I	T	U	R	G	Y	S	A	
P	P	A	R	A	D	I	S	E	O	I	

Matt Swaim is communications coordinator with the Coming Home Network International. He is the cocreator of Sacred Heart Radio/EWTN's *Son Rise Morning Show*, where he served as producer and host.

He earned a bachelor's degree in media communications from Asbury University in 2002. Swaim is the author of three books and has written for a variety of publications, including *Our Sunday Visitor*, *Liguorian*, *Integrated Catholic Life*, and *Catholic Telegraph*. He has appeared on EWTN TV and radio, Relevant Radio, CatholicTV, the Catholic Channel on Sirius/XM Radio and has been a guest host on *Catholic Answers Live*.

Swaim and his wife, Colleen, live with their son in Damascus, Maryland.